DODGE
CHARGER
R/T

BY EMILY ROSE OACHS

BELLWETHER MEDIA • MINNEAPOLIS, MN

Are you ready to take it to the extreme?
Torque books thrust you into the action-packed world
of sports, vehicles, mystery, and adventure. These books
may include dirt, smoke, fire, and dangerous stunts.
WARNING : read at your own risk.

This edition first published in 2017 by Bellwether Media, Inc.

No part of this publication may be reproduced in whole or in part without written permission of the publisher.
For information regarding permission, write to Bellwether Media, Inc., Attention: Permissions Department,
5357 Penn Avenue South, Minneapolis, MN 55419.

Library of Congress Cataloging-in-Publication Data

Names: Oachs, Emily Rose, author.
Title: Dodge Charger R/T / by Emily Rose Oachs.
Other titles: Car Crazy (Minneapolis, Minn.)
Description: Minneapolis, MN : Bellwether Media, Inc., 2017. | Series:
   Torque. Car Crazy | Audience: Ages 7-12. | Includes bibliographical
   references and index.
Identifiers: LCCN 2016036554 (print) | LCCN 2016039199 (ebook) | ISBN
   9781626175785 (hardcover : alk. paper) | ISBN 9781681033075 (ebook)
Subjects: LCSH: Dodge Charger automobile–Juvenile literature. | Dodge
   Brothers–History–Juvenile literature. | Chrysler Corporation–Juvenile
   literature.
Classification: LCC TL215.D6 O23 2016 (print) | LCC TL215.D6 (ebook) | DDC
   629.222/2–dc23
LC record available at https://lccn.loc.gov/2016036554

Editor: Betsy Rathburn   Designer: Brittany McIntosh

Printed in the United States of America, North Mankato, MN.

TABLE OF CONTENTS

A SMOOTH RIDE

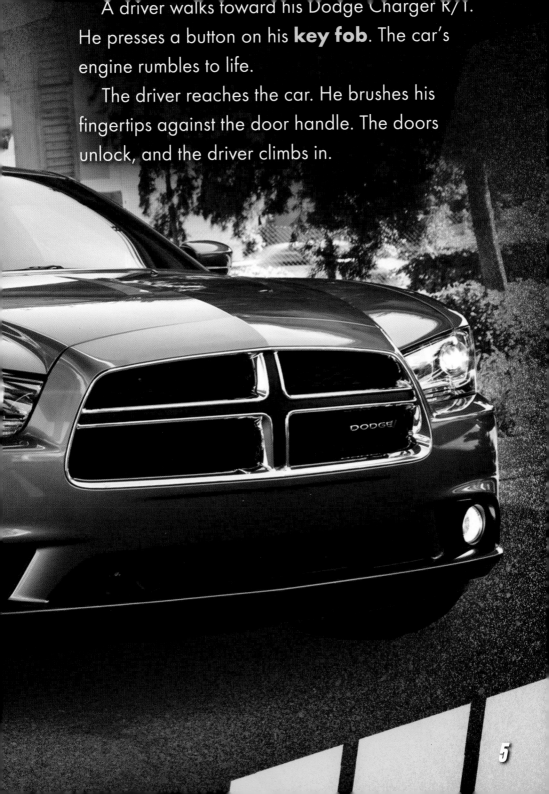

A driver walks toward his Dodge Charger R/T. He presses a button on his **key fob**. The car's engine rumbles to life.

The driver reaches the car. He brushes his fingertips against the door handle. The doors unlock, and the driver climbs in.

The engine growls as the car smoothly **accelerates** onto the road. Inside, the R/T is quiet as it breezes past other cars.

The driver relaxes into his seat with a smile.
The Dodge Charger R/T makes everyday driving
more exciting!

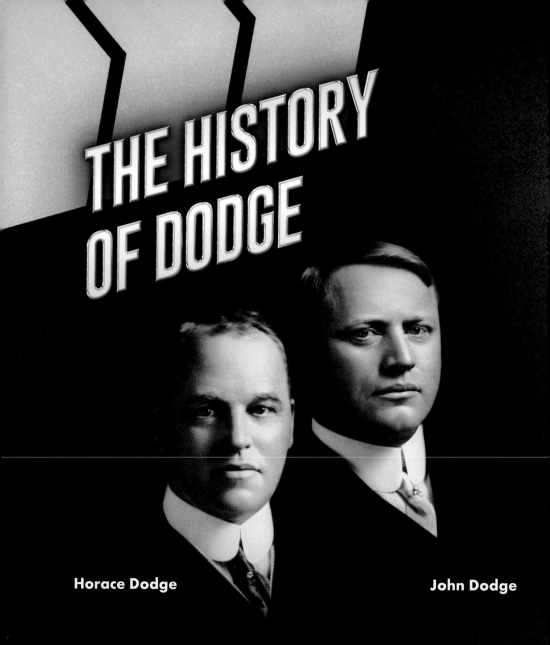

THE HISTORY OF DODGE

Horace Dodge

John Dodge

As children, Horace and John Dodge loved to toy with machines. In 1900, the brothers started making parts for early car companies. They soon built a **reputation** for making **reliable** parts.

By 1914, the brothers were ready for something different. They started creating their own automobiles. Customers loved their cars from the beginning. In just three years, Dodge Motor Company was the fourth-largest carmaker in the country!

GOOD REPUTATION
MORE THAN 13,000 CAR DEALERS ASKED TO SELL DODGE CARS BEFORE THE FIRST EVEN CAME OUT. THE DEALERS ALREADY KNEW THEY COULD TRUST DODGE TO BUILD DEPENDABLE AUTOMOBILES!

Dodge factory

Both brothers passed away in 1920. A bank bought the company from their families a few years later. In 1928, the Dodge Motor Company was sold to Walter P. Chrysler.

Walter P. Chrysler

1966 Dodge Charger

The company made many popular cars over the following years. In 1966, Dodge released the first **generation** Charger. Fans quickly recognized it as a great **muscle car**. Today, Dodge vehicles are still known for their style, quality, and value.

DODGE CHARGER R/T

The Dodge Charger R/T came out in 1968. It offered more power and better performance than the standard Charger.

By 1972, Dodge no longer built the R/T **model**. But in 2006, it returned after more than 30 years. Unlike the old Charger R/T, the new style is a **sedan**. But it still has the heart of a muscle car!

1968 Dodge Charger R/T

2006 Dodge Charger R/T

BEHIND THE NAME

R/T STANDS FOR ROAD AND TRACK. CARS OF THIS TYPE COME WITH STRONGER ENGINES, BETTER SUSPENSION SYSTEMS, AND TOUGHER TIRES. THEY ARE SOME OF DODGE'S BEST-PERFORMING VEHICLES!

TECHNOLOGY AND GEAR

A **V8 engine** powers the Dodge Charger R/T. The car offers excellent **handling** thanks to its top-notch **suspension system**. Using sport mode, drivers can adjust the car's power and steering to give it a race car feel.

Special brake technology gives drivers extra control in the rain. Inserts in the windows keep outside noise from entering the car.

PAINT FROM THE PAST

TODAY, THE CHARGER R/T COMES IN 11 PAINT COLORS FROM THE PAST. THESE COLORS INCLUDE BRIGHT ORANGE, PURPLE, BLUE, AND RED.

hemi V8 engine

FUNNY AND FAST

IN 2014, DODGE SHOWED OFF ITS NEW DODGE CHARGER R/T FUNNY CAR. IT HAS 10,000 HORSEPOWER (7,457 KILOWATTS) AND CAN GO 320 MILES (515 KILOMETERS) PER HOUR!

scallop

The Dodge Charger R/T has a bold shape. Its body is wide and long. Deep **scallops** on the sides were inspired by early Chargers.

The R/T's **power bulge** hood makes room for a large engine. Long-lasting fog lights sit low at the front corners of the car, while a row of taillights stretches across the back.

paddle shifter

Inside, the Charger R/T is sporty and roomy. The front seats have thick cushions along the sides. On the steering wheel, **paddle shifters** give the driver more power over gear changes.

The latest technology lets drivers speak voice commands to change the music or place phone calls. A dashboard touch screen controls the heat, stereo, and other features.

2016 DODGE CHARGER R/T SPECIFICATIONS

CAR STYLE	SEDAN
ENGINE	5.7L HEMI V8
TOP SPEED	145 MILES (233 KILOMETERS) PER HOUR
0 - 60 TIME	5.1 SECONDS
HORSEPOWER	370 HP (276 KILOWATTS) @ 5,250 RPM
CURB WEIGHT	4,280 POUNDS (1,941 KILOGRAMS)
WIDTH	75 INCHES (190 CENTIMETERS)
LENGTH	199.9 INCHES (508 CENTIMETERS)
HEIGHT	58.4 INCHES (148 CENTIMETERS)
WHEEL SIZE	20 INCHES (51 CENTIMETERS)
COST	STARTS AT $33,895

TODAY AND THE FUTURE

The Dodge Charger R/T combines speed and comfort into one sporty sedan. Dodge plans to update the R/T in 2018. Until then, fans continue to drive in style in the current Charger R/T!

HOOD POWER BULGE

DEEP SIDE SCALLOPS

ROW OF TAILLIGHTS

GLOSSARY

accelerates—increases in speed

generation—a version of the same model

handling—how a car performs around turns

key fob—a remote that allows a driver to unlock and start a car

model—a specific kind of car

muscle car—a high-performance sports car with a strong engine

paddle shifters—paddles on the steering wheel of a car that allow a driver to change gears

power bulge—a hump in the hood of a car that makes extra room for a large engine

reliable—trusted to perform well

reputation—the opinion people have about something or someone's character

scallops—indentations on a car's body

sedan—a car with a hard roof and four doors

suspension system—a series of springs and shocks that help a car grip the road

V8 engine—an engine with 8 cylinders arranged in the shape

TO LEARN MORE

AT THE LIBRARY

Blackford, Cheryl. *Powerful Muscle Cars*. North Mankato, Minn.:
Capstone Press, 2015.

Grout, Frank. *Dodge Charger*. Vero Beach, Fla.: Rourke Educational
Media, 2016.

Hamilton, John. *Muscle Cars*. Minneapolis, Minn.: ABDO Pub.,
2013.

ON THE WEB

Learning more about the
Dodge Charger R/T
is as easy as 1, 2, 3.

1. Go to www.factsurfer.com.

2. Enter "Dodge Charger R/T" into the search box.

3. Click the "Surf" button and you will see a list
   of related web sites.

With factsurfer.com, finding more information
is just a click away.

INDEX